New Every Morning

30 Days of Reflection on the
God Opportunities in Each Day

Phil Underwood

Acknowledgments

I want to thank my mother, Maire Phillips Underwood Ph.D., for a lifetime of faith, encouragement and intercession. The views expressed in this collection of reflections are largely because of her life well-lived. I love you, Mom.

I also want to thank Kevin and Paula Tolly for the gift of their home during the pandemic. This transitional abode provided the environment and setting for the daily inspiration and provision of ideas I am sharing with you here. Oh, and you can stay here too for rest, relaxation and days of grace on the Atlantic Ocean in the Beautiful Florida Keys. (Search Facebook for @236Tarpon)

Thank you, Sherry, for believing in me. I love you.

Thank you to my daughter, Alexis Nel, for editorial assistance on choosing the final batch of photos from hundreds. I love you, too.

Phil Underwood, August 2020

INTRODUCTION

Days: they always begin the same; but they are so vastly different.

The earth rotates on its axis eastward and, as it turns, the hidden star we call the sun comes into full and glorious view. The entrance and exit of this star in our twenty-four-hour periods are celebrated the world over. The hours it occupies the sky and the hours we are on the opposite side from it in our rotation have affected our patterns of behavior from the start.

I want to invite you to go with me on a thirty-day exploration of the soul. It's not often you get to travel, explore, experience and learn new things from the stationary positioning that a comfortable place in your home or in a park or in the woods or at the seaside affords but if I did it, you can as well.

On March 16, 2020, President of the United States, Donald Trump issued a directive to the American populace to stay at home, practice social distancing if they were in public and refrain from gatherings of more than ten people.

Two weeks later that directive was extended another thirty days and several states and cities went even farther in their actions to curtail a horrid pandemic that had reached every corner of the world in less than a quarter of a year.

A week later Sherry and I moved into a house owned by friends that sat on the edge of the Atlantic Ocean. I did not realize it, but… *what an opportunity*!

I had already been in a habit of getting up before dawn and reading the ancient texts of Jewish and Christian scripture to both gain knowledge of the history of God and humanity and give context for my own life experiences. I was looking for knowledge and wisdom to expand my life and vision.

As I continued this habit in our beautiful new setting, I was compelled to record a sunrise or two; but one day turned into three and three into eight and before I knew it, I was recording every day's breaking light. Even on the few days that clouds obscured the sun they could not vanquish the dawn's light of opportunity.

So, here we are, you and I, getting ready for Day One of what I hope will be thirty days of renewed sense of joy, confidence, expectation and trust in the God who created Sun and Earth and keeps us in a mysterious balance of gravity and distance, suspended in a vast galaxy in an even larger universe of which we humans cannot find the edge… or the reason for.

So, let us just go with this… evening gave way to morning. That was Day One. Now, on to Day Two. I hope I am preparing you to expect the unexpected. Here is how to address that –

- **Be ready to encounter God.**
- **Look for the subtle opportunities to do so, not the obvious.**
- **Listen for the whispers not the shouts.**
- **Think deeply when you reflect.**
- **Record your thoughts, ideas and moments (this one is REALLY important! Without it you will lose much of your gains.) There are note pages at the back.**
- **Share your experience, no matter how small or seemingly insignificant, with someone every day.**
- **Write me when this is all over and tell me of your thirty days.**

1

God named the light "day" and the darkness "night."
Evening gave way to morning. That was day one.

Genesis 1:5

Evening gives way to morning, again and again. Mornings give opportunity. Mornings offer hope. Mornings are a dread to some and a relief to others.

If you are sleeping really well when the alarm goes off, it's *"Uggggghhhh!"*

If you have tossed and turned all night, it's *"Finally!"*

Or if you are Phil Connors, on a regrettable Groundhog Day assignment in Punxsutawney, Pennsylvania, it's *"Again!?"*

But for everyone, everywhere, morning is when the sun comes up and illuminates the sky. However, it is not the only light.

It is interesting to me that in the Creation account in Genesis 1, everything begins with "Let there be light!" Light appeared. It was not until the fourth day that the sun and reflective moon showed up to give physical manifestations of what was already present.

In our experience every day there is a sunrise. Whether we sleep through it or not, it happens. It says yesterday is gone, tomorrow is not yet here, let us do today.

But the light of the sun in our life is secondary to the light of life in our experience. The sunlight gives us opportunity to **do** (work) but the Light of Life gives us opportunity to **be** (become.)

This book's design is to illuminate each day for you. The daily pages of photographs and thoughts provide opportunity to be influenced by the greater light that never sets, darkens nor can be shrouded by something greater. I want you to see your opportunity. Today we begin.

You do not know what you do not know, but you can always know what you want to know. What do you want to know that you believe only God must know… about you, your life, your destiny, your potential? This is an opportunity for you.

Each day gives way to the next.

Each light beam brightens more than before.

Each sight brings insight.

Let there be light!

2

My heart is committed, O God:
I will sing;
I will sing praises with great affection
and pledge my whole soul to the singing.
Wake up the harp and lyre, and strum the strings;
I will stir the sleepy dawn from slumber!
I will stand and offer You my thanks,
Eternal One, in the presence of others;
I will sing of Your greatness among the nations
no matter where I am.
For Your amazing love soars overhead far into the heavens;
Your truth rises up to the clouds where passing light bends.

Psalm 108:1-5

Singing awakens the dawn.

If you are in a rural farming area or in the Florida Keys, you may hear the crow of a rooster welcoming the day.

If you are in the Tropics you may hear an exotic bird respond to the light of the sun.

If you have a smart phone you may have a favorite tune attached to your alarm to let you know it is time for a new cycle of Earth to enjoy and to join in with.

All around the world song greets the day, both from nature and invention.

The Psalmist here is making a personal commitment to a musical inauguration of the day and he attributes it to an emotional response to God's presence – affection.

His soul – mind, will and emotion – is involved. His movement from slumber to awareness is progressing. His get-out-of-bed action to stand in gratitude for another day is public.

And why? Amazing love, that is why. As amazing as the beams of the sun that stretch into the sky is the truth of God's affection that penetrates the atmosphere holding the earth.

Have you ever begun your day like the Psalmist? I invite you to over the next month. Come to these pages daily and find a reason to reflect on your new day of opportunity, to project your gratitude and to greet the day with faith.

Who knows what the consistent experience may add to your soul, your experience of God and the grace of living.

3

I can find the words that comfort and soothe
the downtrodden, tired, and despairing.
And I know when to use them.
Each morning, it is God who wakes me and tells me
what I should do, what I should say.
Isaiah 50:4

Sometimes I wake up and am stumped. What does this new day hold for me? What should I do? Where should I go? Who should I talk to?

Once, I was in Paris, France, and aimlessly wandering through the Latin Quarter searching for a place to eat dinner on a Sunday night. After being invited into about ten restaurants by hosts standing outside the door entreating customers, I saw someone with a restaurant guide in their hand. It was easy to see they were in the same dilemma as myself – not knowing where to go next.

I asked if their guide held any clues and was responded to curtly and dismissively, "No."

Well, I have never met a conversational challenge that I did not take, so I continued talking as if the response would have been welcoming. The individual was visiting friends in Paris while on holiday from their home in Berlin, Germany. I was in Paris to meet a pastor to talk about international ministry opportunities, having just come from London.

I asked, "If you are visiting friends, where are they?" I was informed that the gentleman of the couple was extremely sick and they had insisted she not spend the evening in Paris cooped up in a house, so here she was fending for herself.

I remarked, "That's odd, the gentleman I am coming to visit is sick as well and I talked to his wife a few hours ago and had my Monday meeting postponed until Tuesday." I mentioned my friends were Americans and she said,

"That's interesting, mine are too."

I asked, "Would your friend's husband happen to be named Mark?" Her jaw dropped.

In a city of 7,000,000 people, two individuals there to visit the same couple happened to be at the same spot at the same time. Not a coincidence, but a God wink. We spent the next two hours sharing stories of life.

Being open to God's presence gives you opportunity to be open to God's purpose & God's surprises. How? Follow the prompts. You will be pleasantly surprised over time at what is happening in you, to you and through you.

Are you open to surprises? Do not look for them, let them arrive.

When they happen, seize the reason.

4 *If I ride on the wings of morning, if I make my home in the most isolated part of the ocean,*
Even then You will be there to guide me; Your right hand will embrace me, for You are always there.
Psalm 139:9-10

I **remember flying from Europe to South Africa on my first sub-equatorial trip in May 2007.** As I crossed the Mediterranean Sea, between midnight and 1:00 am, I looked out the window into the darkness and wrote these words:

> **Paul's domain was the Mediterranean. From Palestine to Lebanon, to Greece, Turkey and eventually Italy. He explored new ways to communicate faith, God and life. In Athens he was the philosopher, in Corinth he was the servant, in Jerusalem he was the advocate, and in Rome he was the writer.**

As I flew over the Mediterranean, I pondered Paul and then I asked, *"God, while I am here, shape my trajectory to be like Paul's. He travelled, started churches, energized people, dealt with incredible challenges, fought off failure, endured horrible seasons of life and was misunderstood in a major way. But he was used by You to recast faith in a new forum."*

Eventually, Paul was a writer. His writing changed lives, and even the world.

Paul traveled, a lot, and everywhere he went he expressed a partnership with Jesus and the Guiding Presence of the Holy Spirit. I am sure, as a good Jewish man, he carried Psalms with him that he used to meditate, worship, reflect and pray.

I imagine him on a ship in the middle of the ocean reading this psalm as the sun burst over the horizon and saying under his breath, *"Father, no matter where I go, there you are. When I am down and out and am emptied of physical resources or when I am flying high and eating the finest foods, I can handle anything because of Christ who infuses his presence into my life. What's next?"*

THAT is being an opportunity seeker!

Will you think about where you are today?

Look around. Is there beauty, blessing, challenge, difficulty, a beginning, an end? What might be your next?

God is there.

You are never alone.

Take a moment and just share your hopes, feelings, adventure desires with him.

He is prepared.

5

The celestial realms announce God's glory;
the skies testify of His hands' great work.
Each day pours out more of their sayings;
each night, more to hear and more to learn.
God stretched out in these heavens a tent for the sun,
and the sun is like a groom who, after leaving his room,
arrives at the wedding in splendor;
He is the strong runner who, favored to win in his race,
is eager to face his challenge.
He rises at one end of the skies and runs in an arc overhead;
nothing can hide from his heat,
from the swelter of his daily tread.

Psalm 19:1-6

nglish winters are gray, cold, damp and easily left behind in favor of spring.

In the spring of 1969, *The Beatles* breakup was imminent. Each man was asserting his individualism and things were cold. George Harrison, skipping a business meeting with his band mates at *Apple Records*, went to Eric Clapton's country home to get away and these lyrics, expressing the anticipation of change in a new day, came from his soul...

Little darling, it's been a long cold lonely winter.
Little darling, it seems like years since it's been here.
Here comes the sun,
Here comes the sun,
And I say, it's all right.
Little darling, the smiles returning to the faces.
Little darling, it seems like years since it's been here.

Sunrise is a metaphor for expectation.

Here the Psalmist acknowledges that the sun is coming as no surprise and the day will be radiantly grand. The day is purposed, the course is planned, the applying of oneself to the opportunity of the day is available. It's a fresh opportunity and it lasts all day long!

If you are coming into the light, it is a great and glorious moment for you to marry the bright opportunity and go forward but it is not vacation. It is opportunity. Turn to God, the Maker of the new day, for guidance coupled with gratitude.

Pray for realistic expectation to marry your idealistic anticipation and...

Enjoy the heat of the sun.

You leave us breathless when Your awesome works answer us
by putting everything right.
God of our liberation—You are the hope of all creation,
from the far corners of the earth to distant life-giving oceans.
With immense power, You erected mountains.
Wrapped in strength, You compelled choppy seas,
crashing waves, and crowds of people
to sit in astonished silence.
Those who inhabit the boundaries of the earth
are awed by Your signs, strong and subtle hints of
Your indelible presence.
Even the dawn and dusk respond to You with joy.

Psalm 65:5-8

Most of us have been in some majestic settings.

Our breath has been taken away at the sight of mountain peaks. Our attention has been captured by white water meeting massive rock formations along sweeping shorelines.

Nature and creation do something for a human soul that no other thing can do; it makes us feel free.

When we escape the concrete roadways, leave the metal cubicles, turn our faces away from lighted screens and enter the most primitive of spaces where no human has constructed a thing, there is a sense of being let out of the ordinary into the extraordinary. Such experience inspires life.

That is the place God most longs for us to be – liberated by the Creator, realizing we are His inimitable creation with as much, or more, brilliance than what we see to create in kind.

You are crowned with glory just as the purple mountain's majesty. You are powerful like the might of the ocean meeting the craggy rocks.

You are awe-inspiring in your likeness to God Himself, something no other created part of this earth can claim.

Today, close your eyes and relive your greatest encounter with nature's immensity. How beautiful is it? How detached from the artificial are you? How unshackled do you feel?

Yes, that is God's opportunity for you to see that in yourself each day. Freedom is your (new) birthright. As the dawn brings newness and the dusk brings rest, live in awe of who you are –

Imago Dei, **the image of God.**

7 *With every sun's rising, surprise us with Your love, satisfy us with Your kindness. Then we will sing with joy and celebrate every day we are alive.*
Psalm 90:1

Every day I know God loves me: some days I pay attention to his winks, hugs and kisses. The days I intentionally revel in His love, He seems to do something to say, "See, I told you so."

Sometimes it is as simple as what happened the other day while sitting on this porch - where all these photos of the sunrise were taken.

I was sitting on the wicker settee on a blue cushion when it happened. A dove came and sat on the cross beam of the porch and just looked at me. It was unnerving at first but after a few seconds it became conversational.

I welcomed the bird, told him that his species was important in Scripture, thanked him for stopping by. Then, he lingered. It was one minute, then two, then four. I am not sure I have seen a bird just hang that long. Another dove joined him, they talked for a few seconds and the visiting dove took off, leaving my friend with me.

I continued to talk to the bird (hey, do not draw any conclusions about my mental health from this story) and express appreciation for his visit. I want to tell you; it was strangely pleasant and very welcome.

I looked down at my work again after a few minutes and when I looked back up, he was gone.

Just like that it was over; but was it?

There was a physical wave of emotional warmth that emanated from what seemed to be the depth of my soul in that moment and I felt a surety that this avian encounter was more than circumstance. I believe that the Creator had these two creations encounter one another in an experience of shared pleasure.

Maybe you have had those experiences, or maybe you have not, when you felt that something beyond the moment orchestrated a divine encounter of a heavenly variety. Some people call these *God winks*. They are opportunities. I call them love.

Here is what I am deeply convinced of: the more we notice things the more we see the love of God and it gives song to our hearts. In fact, and this was not planned, while I was writing this I got up, left the keyboard and experienced a moment and a song came as a response.

This is what I sang…

"Yes, oh, yes, I'm a child of The King, His royal blood now flows through my veins, Oh, I can't deny Him, I will always stand beside Him, Oh, yes, oh, yes, I'm a child of the King." (Yes, I amended the original lyrics to my person.)

Wink!

8 *Yet the way of those who do right is like the early morning sun that shines brighter and brighter until noon.*
Proverbs 4:18

I **enjoy driving**. I will never forget the summer of 2011. It was winter in June in South Africa and I was there to facilitate a workshop helping leaders discover their core values, Biblical identity and their 'Why.'

The workshop was in a remote area in the northern part of the country and I elected to stay two hours away in Pretoria, the capital city, because my daughter was living there and performing in a theatrical company each evening the same week. I was not going to choose between the two. I would do both.

Each morning, before dawn, I would awaken, ready myself and head out in sub-freezing temps to drive north to the workshop.

The drive was routine for the first hour and then it got interesting.

As I meandered off the main highway and onto two-lane roads through sparsely populated areas, I would pass six- and eight-foot high fences to keep wildlife off the highway and out of harm's way.

The brighter the day got the more my eyes were surveying the territory.

On those three cold mornings I routinely saw nyala, impala, maybe an occasional kudu or another antelope-type animal.

My destination, high on a hill overlooking a vast plane would give great views of giraffe, elephants, zebra, wildebeest and other animals I could only see in a zoo in America.

But on that third morning, I was still driving as the sun cleared the horizon behind me and shone the way ahead; and it was as if the rays of light highlighted something unusual.

I could not believe my eyes. It was one of the most elusive of all wild creatures in Africa; the leopard. I pulled my car to the left-hand side of the road and sat to watch. I could feel my pulse in the end of my finger as I clicked the shutter button on my camera.

Soon, the leopard loped away, uninterested in me.

But it was on my way from the darkness of morning to the bright shining of the sun that I made that discovery that day.

And we can all learn from this Scripture one important truth: to discover rarities on the journey to God's bright illumination of life, we have to decide while still in the darkness to get up and move toward and with the light.

How do you discover opportunity? Go forward, letting the light show your way as you go.

Rub the sleep from your eyes, God has an adventure awaiting you.

No telling what you may see this morning in the light.

9 *I hate my life. I have no desire to keep on living. Leave me alone, God, for I have only a short time left. What are these human beings, that You make so much of them— that You shower them with attention? You examine them morning by morning; You test them moment by moment. How long will You stare at me? I can't even clear my throat of spit without an audience.*
Job 7:16-19

Have you read Alexander and the Terrible, Horrible, No Good, Very Bad Day?
Alexander knew that it was going to be a terrible, horrible, no good very bad day. It started with him waking up with the bubble gum that had been in his mouth ending up in his hair. Then he trips on his skateboard and drops his sweater in the sink while the water is running. And that was just the very beginning, BEFORE his breakfast!

Have you had a day like this? Job had several, which led to the complaint above. That last line, regarding Job's awareness of God's presence, is a Biblical classic.

A few years ago, I was supposed to have an incredibly special day. There was nothing that could change what was scheduled that day, but spoilers were abundant.

My first venture out in readiness was to the barber shop. I went to a mall barber and had never seen the gentleman that was my "stylist." I was not too concerned that there was no mirror in front of the chair as I was just getting cleaned up for photo opportunities and to look nice.

Well, never in the history of the world has as much havoc been unleashed on a head of hair as was done in that small shop that day. When I saw what he had done, my first word was *"What?!?!"* He blamed it on my seven cowlicks. *Hmmph!*

After that, I got the wrong food order and could not express my frustration to anyone. I got into a war with my spouse. I was demoralized and humiliated by another person who I did not think I could please if I had written a check for a million dollars. And, finally, a person I had asked to be a centerpiece of my special occasion showed up in jeans, so-so shoes and a plaid shirt instead of a proper suit.

And, my troubles did not compare to Job's. God is not taking an opportunity for troubling you.

I tend to credit God's displeasure with me when things go wrong. This is what Job's friends believed and told him incessantly. I know better and have since learned much deeper realities about God's incessant love, brilliant view of my personhood and never-ending support.

Do you have ideas that God is in control of the bad things and that He is right up there on your shoulder wagging His finger in shame even when you want to spit? Well, He is not. Today, revel in the reality that God is ever-present, but not to scowl and hiss. He just likes to be close to you. Look for Him, over your shoulder, any time today. **He is there, smiling broadly.**

10 *I lie down at night and fall asleep.*
I awake in the morning—healthy, strong, vibrant—
because the Eternal supports me.
No longer will I fear my tens of thousands of enemies
who have surrounded me!

David, on the run from his son, Psalm 3:5-6

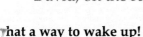**What a way to wake up!**

Can you imagine? Opening your eyes every day, despite what is going on around you, healthy, strong and vibrant - it must be an amazing blessing.

What if this kind of life begins in trust, not circumstance?

What a bold and bodacious statement David makes here, *"No longer will I fear my tens of thousands of enemies who have surrounded me."*

David is King of Israel but his son, Absalom, wants to be. In fact, Absalom subverted his father's authority and gained favor to the point that he asserted himself as King and his dad, David, fled. It is in this period, living like a hunted and wounded soul, that he writes this song containing his confidence in God despite his situation.

Have you ever had 'contrary confidence'? I just made that phrase up and I like it. The Bible is filled with people who had it – a confidence and assurance of good things happening when there was no physical evidence that they should?

Abraham epitomizes this when the Bible reports *"Hoping in spite of hopeless circumstances, he believed that he would become "the father of many nations…"*

The contradiction to hope is fear – the expectation of nothingness or worse. A lot of people find themselves in fear, worry and anxiety when they wake up every morning. Why do so many people expect to be worse off than better off? To diminish, not increase? To lose, not win? It's because they may not see the opportunity each day affords as a gift from God.

I want you to join me in a difference-making waking every day -

healthy, strong and vibrant!

How might we do this?

Be immersed in the language, messages, instruction, and truth regarding God's love. John, the loved friend of Jesus, wrote for our benefit, *"Where God's love is, there is no fear, because God's perfect love takes away fear."*

So, if we want to wake up HEALTHY, STRONG, VIBRANT, while not fearing tens of thousands of enemies, we need to know God loves us, is crazy about us and that He planted our lives IN Christ, the most beloved one of all. That way we KNOW we cannot be separated from His love. As Paul experienced, *"I have every confidence that nothing—not death, life, heavenly messengers, dark spirits, the present, the future, spiritual powers, height, depth, nor any created thing—can come between us and the love of God revealed in the Anointed, Jesus our Lord."*

Look forward to tomorrow morning's opportunity. Wait, just begin today!

11

In the morning, O Eternal One, listen for my voice; in the day's first light, I will offer my prayer to You and watch expectantly for Your answer.

Psalm 5:3

was twenty-five years old, but I felt like I was eight. It was a day I had long looked forward to and when the sun went down the night before I knew it was next up. My dad had organized a deep-sea fishing trip with some of my friends who were NFL players for the *Atlanta Falcons*.

We drove on Friday from Atlanta to Panama City, Florida to arrive in time for a great seafood feast. Then we retired to our hotel to sit around, share stories, tell jokes and generally just enjoy a guy night. By 10:00 pm we were ready to head to our rooms and turn out the lights for a 5:00 am wake up call. (Remember when hotels did that?)

Well, the anticipation was huge for me. I had never been more than a few yards offshore and to think we were going so far as to not see land was exhilarating for me. Finally, the phone rang, and it was time for us to get up, dress quickly, get a diner breakfast and a coffee to go and head to the docks by 6:00 am for departure.

The day was everything I could have hoped for and more. We caught grouper, snapper, a couple of grunts, a puffer fish and encountered a few barracuda who appreciated our bringing our catch through their pathways so that they could take them from us.

Eventually, too soon if you ask me, it struck high noon and we headed back on our two-hour return trip to reality. But the thing that stays with me to this day, more than thirty years later, is the anticipation, the expectation of something good happening beyond the sunrise.

I did not plan and give *myself* this day, my dad did.

I have become convinced that our Heavenly Father is infinitely energized to bless us as much and more than good, earthly fathers. In fact, five times in the New Testament, there is a direct quote about how God takes pleasure in giving us the elements that make life enjoyable.

Jesus taught us to pray, "*Father, Your will be done on Earth as in Heaven.*" There is a direct correlation between discovering God's gifts of pleasure for us, invoking them in prayer and then anticipating them.

What are you convinced that God wants you to experience today? Abundance, prosperity, wisdom, health, love – all are His pleasure to give. Jesus said ask, so that your heart will be filled with joy. James, Jesus' brother, said "the reason you do not possess God's will is that you haven't asked for God's will." Many of us are content to trust ourselves over God but that is not the opportunity extended to us by this gracious Heavenly Father.

Today, make a list as Paul instructs us to do, and tell God what you see is His pleasure to give you and thank Him along with the asking.

Why? It's as good as done.

The boat will leave the dock just as Dad promised it would.

*Rescue me! Save me, O my God, from my enemies; set me in a
safe place, far above any who come to attack me...
Those brutes are aligned, ready to attack me for no good cause,
my Eternal One. I have not crossed them.
I've done nothing wrong, yet they rush ahead to start the
assault...
But me? I will sing of Your strength. I will awake with the sun
to sing of Your loving mercy
Because in my most troubled hour, You defended me.
You were my shelter.*

Psalm 59:1-4, 16

Bullies. intimidators. manipulators. Oppressors. Mean people.

Some of us have had more trouble than necessary. When I was in ninth grade I had trouble, or rather a troublesome person, who thought his calling was to make my life miserable, embarrass me in front of peers, assert his seniority over me in an extracurricular activity group and generally, just feel good about himself lording over a freshman neophyte.

This was an unnecessary thing for him to do because I mostly placed myself at the end of the line in my dedication, performance and honing of my musical skills. In our Douglas County High School *Marching Tigers Band*, each instrument grouping ranked from best to least based on audition. I was a proud trombone player and I ranked ninth among eight.

I thought about asserting myself and putting the 'Big Man on Campus' in his place but it would not have ended well in my own authority, strength and might. I am sure you have had problematic moments, seasons, years.

It does not have to be a person that is against you, sometimes it feels like the world has become an enemy. Months have more days than you have money. Jobs have more demands than you have skills. Relationships are draining instead of uplifting. The doctor tells you that something inside, that you cannot see or control, is eating away at your ability to live well, if at all.

This is where trouble becomes an opportunity.

In all the above, or any of the above, God is present and attentive. He is saying, "Don't forget Me. Ask me in. I have something you do not have – power over everything." I love what the Apostle Paul said, in what was probably his GREATEST flow of words ever, "*If God is for us, who (what) can be against us?*" And, look at the attitude modeled for us to follow... Get beyond the trouble and sing about God's stronger-ness! Get up EARLY to croon about God's mercy-full action. You've got an ace in the hole, a got-your-back God, a Dad who watches His kids.

Boast in your God.

13 *How good it is to give thanks to the Eternal*
and to praise Your name with song, O Most High;
To speak of Your unfailing love in the morning
and rehearse Your faithfulness as night begins to fall.
Psalm 92:1-2

Stories, they are the essence of our lives. I love to think about all the experiences I have had, whether challenging or celebratory and even in between. When I look at my life I have so many intersections with God it seems like He is everywhere, all the time, morning and night. Some of the memories, from the earliest to the most recent, that are chapters in my story are…

- At four years old seeing my mom taken to, and then visiting her in, the hospital. This was the week that President Kennedy was assassinated in Dallas, Texas and I have clear video recall of this impacting week. She was affected with a disease known as Guillain-Barre Syndrome, a rare disorder in which the body's immune system attacks the nerves. She was paralyzed from her throat down. At one point during her hospitalization, the doctors told my dad that Mom would not live through the night. When she did, they said that she'd never walk again. She did. She is still walking at 81, more than fifty-five years later.

- When I was 17, I had the privilege of singing in a church youth choir that won national acclaim. The summer, in fact the morning, after graduating high school, we toured the East Coast of the United States. In Charlotte, North Carolina, we were performing at a church when I was overwhelmed with a supernatural experience. I felt a presence come upon me from head to toe. This feeling defies description to this day but every time I dwell on it, like now, I can relive the experience in micro fashion. During that experience I heard a word in my gut. That is the only way I know how to describe it - a word was in me, not in my ears but in my being. That word? *Preach.* I did not know what to do with it but time has borne out the process of becoming a proclaimer of God's message story.

- I was 27 when another experience happened (and I am skipping several.) My father had the unfortunate event of a flat tire in a truck one day about 30 minutes from his home. Without a spare, he needed to get the tire off, take it to be repaired and then return to put it back on the wheel and continue his way. He called me to help. When I arrived, he already had the tire off so we loaded it in my truck and found a repair shop. Within 20 minutes the tire was ready to go and an employee from the shop offered to follow us and put it back on the wheel. While that happened, I was sitting in the cab of the truck reading a magazine when I heard words in my being again. It was simple - "*Phil, I want to show you My world.*" That night I called the only person I knew living outside the USA. His name was Jim and he said, "This is so strange, I was in my office this morning (happened to be at the same time I was in the truck) and I felt I should call you and invite you to join my team opening up ministry training centers in Caribbean countries and Latin America. I did and a million miles later I am still visiting God's world.

I guess I could fill up an entire book with the opportunities of His unfailing love (provision, care and attention) and his great faithfulness from dawn until the night, waiting to do it again tomorrow. **How about you?**

I wake before the dawn and call for help; I hope in Your words.
Psalm 119:147

 ELP!!!!!

How many times has that been the extent of my prayer life? You too?

But, after I yell, beg, bargain and cajole, I mostly wonder when the other shoe will fall.

Why? I talked myself into low expectations to avoid high disappointments.

Now, I have had some spectacular answers to prayer, but I have learned that it is primarily because I am confident in God's Word, not just emptily wishing for good outcomes. Knowing what God's will is for my well-being and forward motion, then being aware of my purpose and primary reason for living, gives me great confidence.

The lyric above, from an ancient Jewish hymn, is from the longest ever recorded. Each verse in this hymn starts with a successive letter of the alphabet, like A to Z. Each verse is about the value of knowing God's words, His expression of life, love, commitment and design toward humanity.

Look at the line and imagine the life of the writer, "Wow, this is going to be a challenging day. I have deadlines, demands, doubts about my ability to cover, debts to pay and delivering on it all is beyond me." So, what does he do? He gets ahead of it.

The pray-er wakes before dawn.

The pray-er realizes his human limitations but knows he has a relationship with God, and he knows God's way. However, the way immediately in front is a challenge… an opportunity for grit, resolve and help from within.

The pray-er calls on God's intervention, assistance and bigger-ness. Then, the dawn breaks the night and the pray-er begins, *expecting* his opportunity to be met with God's partnership.

Why does the pray-er expect? He knows what God has said about him, promised him, helped him envision about his life and how it brings God 'good pleasure' to be trusted and believed.

The word 'hope' is a feeling for a preferred outcome based on expectation. I expect God to do what He said, be who He said, act like He said. Wishes are the same, preferring a different outcome, but not expecting it.

One thing we are never encouraged to do in spiritual development, as we are growing in our relationship with God, is to ignore that we have His destiny on our life. As the writer of **Ecclesiastes** says, '*we have eternity in our hearts.*' We are to seek it out, find guidance toward it, pursue it and then see God do his part.

But, if I do not know God's will, all I can do is wish. I just want, wait to see what happens. Friend, that is not hope and it never lends itself to developing faith, beyond what God can to what God will. Seize the opportunity to face challenging days with prayer-filled faith.

So, do not wait until the morning of the challenge. Know, discover, learn what God says about giving you abundant life now and find the path to life.

Then, you will expect when you get up early to set your day in alignment with the heart of God.

15 *A fast for Me involves sharing your food*
with people who have none,
giving those who are homeless a space in your home,
giving clothes to those who need them,
and not neglecting your own family.
Then, oh then, your light will break out like the warm,
golden rays of a rising sun; in an instant, you will be healed.
Your rightness will precede and protect you;
the glory of the Eternal will follow and defend you.
Then when you do call out, "My God, where are You?"
The Eternal One will answer, "I am here, I am here."

Isaiah 58:7-9

Imagine walking the beach before dawn. With care, hurt, sickness or confusion slamming against the walls of your mind. You can see forever across to the horizon and beyond, but you feel closed in, arrested, chained to the malady that seems to define your existence right now.

Before you know it the glow of the impending sunrise begins to lighten the sky, the sand below your feet and the waves moving the tide to and from the shoreline.

And, then, instantaneously, it's more than a glow, it's a beam! You feel the warmth, the life, the brightness crash into your eyes like it wants to get in.

And, suddenly, before you know it, things seem different. That weighing problem, confusion, doubt, evaporates like the morning dew under the warmth of the breaking sun over the horizon.

How does that happen for a person? Well, the Prophet Isaiah, speaking to humans at their core, is telling us something. He is telling us that God, in His core, wants to be our Provider – food, shelter, clothing – and He wants to be our constant Companion as well as our Defender. And the caveat is to sense his provision and protection: just go ahead and be like Him.

If God provides and protects, you provide and protect.

If God welcomes and embraces, you welcome and embrace. If God loves…wait, if God IS love, you BE love.

He is here. He is here!

What an opportunity, to experience and to be.

Where do you need God to show up for you today? He may do it through people, circumstances, intervention. So, in faith and confidence that God is who He says He is, you be who He says you are – as Christ is, so are you in this world.

Show up for someone.

16 *How enduring is God's loyal love;*
the Eternal has inexhaustible compassion.
Here they are, every morning, new!
Your faithfulness, God, is as broad as the day.
Lamentations 2:22-23

I feel it.
Failure, or the emotive feeling of failure, has engulfed me at times.

I will never forget a moment like this, among too many, when I observed a situation and allowed someone to do something that was not for their benefit in any sense of the word.

I stood by stoically and remained silent because I felt that I would somehow benefit by their ignorance and lack of a complete understanding of details and circumstances.

As I turned away from this experience and went my way I was engulfed in remorse, shame and regret that I had not done something, said something, interjected what I knew into the moment.

My Lord, I needed mercy. And, that is just ONE of my scenarios of foolish decision and negative action.

Mercy is that spiritual force and movement that absolves us from paying the penalty of human indifference, willful rebellion, and conscious inaction. But, unfortunately, mercy does not inoculate us against selfishness and greed and manipulation. We can get mercy in the morning and need it again within hours.

Mercy stands up, points to our misgiving and misdeeds, and says "I do not condemn you [give you just punishment and judgment,] but I do say I see the accusation and the reality of evidence before us and I am giving you a way to go beyond your guilt." What an opportunity!

Mercy, says "Look ahead but also look forward." You may think those are similar and they may be, but mercy wants you to take your eyes off the past – look ahead – progressively – look forward – preventing you from making the same misdeed again. Just think, new day is new life.

How? Through the nature of God, the mercy giver. His nature has three life-affirming and possibility-giving dynamics that we would do well to be thoroughly acquainted with…

- Loyal Love – it is the very essence of who God is. He cannot *not* love you.
- Inexhaustible Compassion – he *feels* your feelings and doesn't just look at your behaviors.
- Daily Faithfulness – to us and then primarily to who He is because He will not be anything other.

So, my advice, don't live a life where you let others crash or where you let yourself do wrong and you pretend it doesn't matter. It does. But God steps in when you are aware and inviting. Like the woman brought to Jesus, caught in some deadly sin trap, he says, ***"I do not condemn you. Go and sin no more."*** 'Go' is the invitation to this opportunity.

17 *Sing to the Eternal of all the good things He's done.*
Bless His name; broadcast the good news of
His salvation each and every day.
Psalm 96:2

I remember a song we sang when I was young that I have not heard in years. The lyrics went like this…

When upon life's billows you are tempest tossed,
When you are discouraged, thinking all is lost,
Count your many blessings name them one by one,
And it will surprise you what the Lord has done.

Chorus:
Count your blessings, name them one by one;
Count your blessings, see what God has done;
Count your blessings, name them one by one,
Count your many blessings, see what God has done.

Are you ever burdened with a load of care?
Does the cross seem heavy you are called to bear?
Count your many blessings, every doubt will fly,
And you will keep singing as the days go by.

So amid the conflict, whether great or small,
Do not be discouraged, God is over all;
Count your many blessings, angels will attend,
Help and comfort give you to your journey's end.

When I hear those lyrics, I can see my dad leading his church in singing while my mother is playing the Wurlitzer organ. This song was on page 339. It was more than a song, it was an invitation much like the verse above. I hope you will sit with this for a few minutes, read, listen, do.

Interact with the lyrics as if it is conversing with you. Consider the questions, the encouragement, the invitation. As you begin this day singing and God joins you as you go, then determine to tell someone. Make a post on social media, email a friend, phone a family member, and tell people this about your rich experience. What an opportunity to share your story.

Care to watch or listen? https://bit.ly/ReflectOnBlessings

18 *We have a fuller confirmation of the message of the prophets. You would do well to pay close attention to this word; it is like a light that shines for you in the darkness of night until the day dawns when the morning star rises in your own hearts.*
2 Peter 1:19

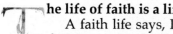

The life of faith is a life of FAITH.

A faith life says, I am going to live my life based on a belief. From that foundation of belief my decisions, assumptions, lifestyle, relationships, career, money, service, appetites, pursuits and pleasure will be governed by ideals I learn from the One who invited me to put my faith in him.

This person is Jesus, the Christ. I believe He was and is 100% human, born of a woman that was divinely impregnated in a divinely miraculous conception. This woman, that I know as Mary, had to have this same kind of faith – trusting her entire life and risking her human reputation to an unbelievable and unenviable task – to carry the one and only birthed human without the seed of man, instead having the seed of a supernatural God.

You say what?

To trust something that begins so untenably is a huge leap. I trust a man who died and that I believe now lives, resurrected from the dead and seen by hundreds before leaving Earth for heaven. In heaven, He represents me, advocates for me, prays for me and possesses my life as if it were His own. He does not care for himself above me. He does not love himself above me. He does not protect himself above me. In fact, I believe that in Him I exist in a new dimension, I am animated and made alive by His spirit and I find my true self identity.

Peter, a friend and follower of Jesus died because of Jesus. In fact, he was crucified as Jesus was with one exception. He demanded to be killed head down and feet up to say that he honored the man who gave him life, purpose and eternity.

In this short piece of his writings to other followers of Jesus Christ, people who also trusted his life and love for them, he referred to the prophets of ancient times that spoke futuristically of Jesus. Their word was gold, these prophets. But Peter says, "We experienced what the prophets only saw in visions and dreams. I am confirming to you that everything they wrote, I saw. I ate with him. I was forgiven by him. I was restored by him."

Then he said, "Pay attention to everything I, and others who were with him, say about him. It will come to you gradually. You do not just arrive a full faith and trust in one day, but begin in your faith life with a small crack of dawn illumination, then let it grow in you as you experience him for yourself. Your faith will grow from that little sliver of sun that breaks across the horizon of your soul until it is full-blown high noon brightness and then, then you will know that your faith – a belief that gives both boundary and infinity to your life – is the most real thing you possess."

Your opportunity, if you accept it... Believe. Trust. Rely.

Follow… you'll be bright!

19

Sing, all you who remain faithful!
Pour out your hearts to the Eternal with praise and melodies;
let grateful music fill the air and bless His name.
His wrath, you see, is fleeting, but His grace lasts a lifetime.
The deepest pains may linger through the night,
but joy greets the soul with the smile of morning.
David, Psalm 30:4-5

You have a story of a long night. In fact, your night may have felt like what you could describe as a dark night of the soul. For most people it is a difficult, dry, spiritually empty time from which you would give anything to escape. There is no rule that says you cannot identify troubled seasons or desert places as such, but the originator of the idea saw it as an intentional and progressive experience.

St John of the Cross, a 16th Century poet and mystic follower of Jesus, created two separate works in this theme and both were about a purposeful pilgrimage within.

The first work, eight stanzas of five lines each, translated from Spanish, begins:

> *In an obscure night*
> *Fevered with love's anxiety*
> *(O hapless, happy plight!)*
> *I went, none seeing me*
> *Forth from my house, where all things quiet be*

In commenting on his work, St John describes his journey. "In this first verse, the soul tells the mode and manner in which it departs, as to its affection, from itself and from all things, dying through a true mortification to all of them and to itself, to arrive at a sweet and delicious life with God."

His soul is seizing an opportunity to explore, experience and then exult.

So, the dark night does not always have to be a negative, although we know that it sometimes is.

Whenever you do find yourself in the dark, the Psalmist instructs us in moving through it and beyond it to God's entrance into our experience. How? You sing. Music is the medium.

We know that, because of Jesus, the wrath of God has been satisfied for us – we do not have to be scared that God's gonna get us. On the upside, grace (spiritual strength supplied by God to us) is a gift to get us through painful experiences to joy, just the same as night ends with the dawn.

That kind of opportunity, found in a new day, is music to our ears.

Go ahead, do it now, sing God a song.

20 *In your short run of days, have you ever commanded the*
morning to begin or taught the sun to rise in its place?
Under your watch has the early light ever taken hold of
the earth by the edges and shaken the wicked loose?
Under dawn's early light the earth takes shape as does clay
when a seal is firmly pressed in it; Its colors and features
stand out as a well-made garment does from the body.
God to Job 38:12-14

Sometimes I think I know better than God what I need and how to supply it. In those times I don't tell Him, I just do it. Later, if it doesn't go well, I sheepishly approach Him, prayerfully of course, and let Him in on the secret... things did not go too well for me there.

You may know the story of Job. It may be the world's oldest story, predating the compilation of the story of human beginnings in Genesis. It is the story of this just and righteous man who God respected and had so much faith and trust in that he allowed evil to encircle him, steal from him, take away his family in death and destroy everything under his ownership.

Job's friends looked at this picture-perfect man and decided there had to be a reason. Isn't there always a reason that things go bad?

Not necessarily. In fact, our limited knowledge of life, always subjective to our experience is apt to lead us astray. That is where God comes in, and as with Job, he offers His perspective, His wisdom, His knowledge and His partnership with each and every individual human.

And how does He advertise His experience and offer? He asks us if we have His credentials.

He commands the day's entry
He taught the sun to rise in its place
He lights the corners of the earth exposing those who operate in the dark
He reveals the shape of life and imprints Himself in our life
He gives the color to our life that gives us our unique and inimitable style

But, if we do not acknowledge his greater greatness, thinking it all depends on us, we begin to measure our life in terms of failure or success of our circumstances. That is not the greater way.

When challenging, even negative, circumstances happen in our life, step back, look up, ask for guidance and depend on the One who sees and knows it all to inform our seeing and knowing in the moment. God says, *'Take the opportunity to ask Me. I'm approachable.'*

It will order life in an entirely new dimension.

21 *Early in the morning, Jesus got up, left the house while it was still dark outside, and went to a deserted place to pray. Simon and the others traveling with Jesus looked for Him. They finally tracked Him down.*

People: *Everybody wants to know where You are!*

Jesus: *It's time we went somewhere else—the next village, maybe—so I can tell more people the good news about the kingdom of God. After all, that's the reason I'm here.*

Mark's biography of Jesus 1:35-38

What do you do early in the morning?

Yes, that's what I thought, you go sloooooooowly.

Jesus, and this is my personal theory, was the last person in the world who would need to pray. He was God, so in a way, it just confounds me. Not only that He would pray, but that we are told on multiple occasions that prayer - early, consistent, passionate prayer - was His daily priority.

I have attended talks about prayer, read books about prayer, seen people pray loud prayers and pray quietly. However, the most I have ever learned about prayer I learned by praying.

At another place in the biographical stories of Jesus he is quoted as saying He was just simply doing what the Father showed Him and saying what the Father spoke to Him. I can only come to the conclusion that He received divine communication in prayer.

I remember being a very young man, just two weeks shy of my 21st birthday, and trying to make the hardest decision of my life up until that time – I did not know what to do, how to do it or when I would get to a point of decision – so I got up and went to pray. I got away from everyone and into a place where no one could hear me, in the middle of a field used for sports. I remember it until this day, as if it were a video playing on the screen of my mind. When I walked out of that field that day, I just knew what to do.

I can imagine Jesus pioneering that experience for me. He got up, went to pray where no one could easily locate him and He did not just talk, he listened. It was His practice. Now, in my second half century on Earth, I follow that same pattern – early, intentional, alone and listening.

I said earlier that my best teacher on prayer was praying. I want to re-emphasize that now. Just pray. And, in your praying, listen. One of my mentors used to say to me and others that one of the highest forms of prayer is listening. I can attest to that.

Before we go today, look at the end of this little story… Jesus had a plan coming out of that early morning priority: living His purpose.

This morning don't rush off. Stay for a few minutes, listening.

You will get something about where you are going today and why.

Make it count.

Despite [the failure of religion and the religious],
the Eternal One is right there in her midst;
nothing He does is wrong.
Every morning He delivers His judgment;
He illuminates the right way to live.
Though, like the sun, He never fails to appear, it's amazing
that the lawbreakers aren't ashamed of their actions.

The Jewish prophet, Zephaniah 3:5-6

Every day.

I have not been the same every day of my life. In fact there have been seasons when I was quite contrary to my reputation, how people knew me and how I wanted to live and know myself.

I remember a season when I represented a God and a version of myself that were contrary to what I now know and experience. I remember tears streaming down my face during this song because it seemed so right but I felt so wrong. I heard the lyrics, week after week, as they spoke to my heart…

Light of the world
You stepped down into darkness
Opened my eyes, let me see
Beauty that made this heart adore You
Hope of a life spent with You
Here I am to worship
Here I am to bow down
Here I am to say that You're my God
You're altogether lovely
Altogether worthy
Altogether wonderful to me
Well, I'll never know how much it cost
To see my sin upon that cross…

The presence and proximity of God came to me again and again to say, "Phil, your way is not working is it? You are avoiding truth but here I am holding out an olive branch of peace for you. Until you allow my light into your darkness and submit your will to My higher knowledge and authority you will never get it right. I am offering you a new day of opportunity, the better way to live your life – in love, not fear."

I am offering you a new day of opportunity, the better way to live your life – in love, not fear.

When I shamefully admitted ignoring God, then I saw a way forward in loving forgiveness, acceptance and relationship. What, in your life, doesn't hold up in light of God's wisdom and knowledge? Give it up. Worship Him over yourself. **See the light and walk the way.**

23

He will spread out righteousness for you as a sunrise spreads radiance over the land; He will deliver justice for you into the light of the high sun.
Psalm 37:6

ne of the things I like most about the sunrise is the imperceptible addition of light, second by second, prior to the entrance of the star over the horizon of the sea. The anticipation grips me.

Is it now? *(Wait.)* Is it now? *(Wait.)* Is it now? *(Wait.)* Then I glance down, or away, for a second or two, and when I look back, **BOOM!** It is **NOW!** The light that was ever-so-gradually filling the dark canvas with light blue hues has now been joined by a radiant heat that I feel on my face. Then the remainder of the star emerges from beneath the sea's edge and things begin to animate.

I hear traffic a few blocks away zipping up and down US 1. I am at Mile Marker 91.6 of this ribbon of road that can hold transport traveling anywhere between Mile Marker 0 in Key West, Florida and Mile Marker 2,369 in Fort Kent, Maine.

I see boats leaving shore to venture into the Atlantic Ocean, soon to cross America's only living coral barrier reef a couple of miles to the east. Some are moving for vocation, some for avocation and some on vacation. People are moving and days are beginning.

As the day brightens visibility increases, learning heightens, production revs up and experiences happen. Today's thought brings us to God's credible grace and love for us. He is our Defender, Protector and Advocate. He is a God of justice. That does not mean that everything turns out rosy, but in your heart it means God knows and in his court of decision you are clear, clean and collected to him.

What is your injustice? Have you ever been falsely accused? You are the only person who knows the truth, but everyone assumes you are just trying to cover for yourself. It is maddening.

Have you been misunderstood, and everything you say or do to try to remedy the disconnection, is like trying to grow flowers in concrete?

Have you been robbed of your job at a time when you need it more than ever and it just isn't fair, easy, or an indicator of the value of your ethics, skill or quality of the production you give.

Has the person you love quit loving you and it just does not make sense. You have laughed together, cried together, shared life together, traveled together, slept together. They have seen every part of you and now they are rejecting you. Are you not good enough, attractive enough, smart enough?

Where do you go? What do you do? You let the sun come up on a new tomorrow, that is what you do. Because in that new day the God of your heart and soul is creating new opportunity, connection, truth about who you really are and advertising your gifts and value to people who will see you for what you are – brilliant, beautiful and bodacious.

Watch the sunrise the day after that sundown on what was.

Let Him make it right. You do not have to.

So we have no reason to despair. Despite the fact that our outer humanity is falling apart and decaying, our inner humanity is breathing in new life every day. You see, the short-lived pains of this life are creating for us an eternal glory that does not compare to anything we know here.
Paul, 2 Corinthians 4:16-17

have heard it called 'the daily grind,' but what do you call it?

There is a Latin proverb, only two words in length, *Nascentes morimur,* that roughly translates as "Being born, we are dying." At some point Gautama Buddha wrote, "We begin to die from the moment we are born, for birth is the cause of death. The nature of decay is inherent in youth, the nature of sickness is inherent in health, in the midst of life we are verily in death." And, Janne Teller wrote, "From the moment we are born, we begin to die."

Those quotes and sentiments pale in comparison to the "each new day provides new life" ideas that Paul shares in his writing, inspired by the will and Spirit of God. There is an honest understanding of the nature of our natural state, but there is a supernatural offering from God's heart that lifts, encourages and plants hope in my heart for tomorrow.

It comes to a place of disposition. Are you more inclined to the physical world of understanding life and opportunity or the spiritual Kingdom of God that flips the script and offers enrichment, possibility and increase on any given day of our life?

Going back into the ancient texts of Scripture we see God's heart for the experience of human life communicated again and again. I want to invite you to just read these passages in light of opportunity and, after each one, soak in the voice of God's Spirit speaking it deeply into your soul psyche beginning this day…

"I gave you the choice today between life and death, between being blessed or being cursed. Choose life, so that you and your descendants may live!" - God, Deuteronomy 30.19

"…my life is abundant—like a lush olive tree cared for at the house of the one True God. I put my trust in His kind love forever and ever; it will never fail." - David, Psalm 52.8

"The thief approaches with malicious intent, looking to steal, slaughter, and destroy; I came to give life with joy and abundance." - Jesus, John's account of Jesus' life, 10.10

"His divine power has given us everything we need to experience life and to reflect God's true nature through the knowledge of the One who called us by His glory and virtue. Through these things, we have received God's great and valuable promises, so we might escape the corruption of worldly desires and share in the divine nature." – Peter, his second teaching letter, 2 Peter 1.3

"A mind focused on the flesh is doomed to death, but a mind focused on the Spirit will find full life and complete peace." – Paul, letter to Roman followers of Jesus, 8.6

So, today, capture the opportunity for life! And pray to the Father with confidence!

25

What you witness now will be very different—a new day when seeds of peace will be sown in fertile soil. The seeds will grow into sheaves of wheat, and the vines will produce luscious grapes. The ground will yield its crops, and pleasant dew will again fall from the heavens. And I will give these things to My remnant as their inheritance.
Zechariah, a Jewish prophet 6th century BC, 8:1-2

"Those were the days my friend,
We thought they'd never end
We'd sing and dance forever and a day
We'd live the life we choose,
We'd fight and never lose
For we were young and sure to have our way"

Eventually, it seems, everything left to us degenerates. This lively, happy-sounding song has a lamenting tone that is wistful for what *was* because what *is* does not seem as good.

But, with God, it can be quite the opposite in our own daily journeys!

In the historical context of this passage, God's family of Israel has disregarded his guidance, forgotten him and gone their own way. They have ended up as exiled servants, far from home, in another nation.

God, who knows the end from the beginning, had already told Israel, through the young prophet Jeremiah, that he had plans for them. He told them this when they were at rock bottom, far from home in that exile, completely controlled by a foreign power and in slavery. The plans, God said, were for good and not evil. The plans included hope for a new future. Now, years later, Israel is back at home and God has a message… It's a new day!

What is it that, getting up this morning, you do not want to be a part of your life anymore? What is it that may have bound you, enslaved you, oppressed you and just plain ol' bothered you? Have you felt 'out of place' where you did not belong. Well, when you, like Israel, are fed up with being fed up, sick and tired of being sick and tired… Tell God you are ready for the opportunity to be 'home' where he sees that you belong.

Take a note pad, list what you want to leave behind and then what you want to see in this promise: a promise that arises from an earlier promise about a hope-filled future. What's your preferred destination?

When you arrive (today?) be ready for fertile soil, seeds of peace, abundant production and luscious fruit to turn into new wine. This is the opportunity that God provides.

That is God's way of desire for you, living in Christ.

At night I long for You with all that is in Me.
When morning comes, I seek You with all my heart.
For when Your justice is done on earth, then everyone in
the world will learn righteousness.
Isaiah 26:8-9

Desire is an internal emotionally-charged energy. Desire is what fuels a passionate pursuit of something that is out of your reach in the natural but not out of the realm of Divine possibility.

What do you desire? Many people desire profitability while others desire emotional and soul connection in love. Some people desire an experience, destination, possession, or position. Desire allows us the privilege of dissatisfaction and feeling yet unfulfilled.

Desire is only borne of the frustration of the not yet. There is a vast minority of people who wonder about a desire for God. Why? I think it is because God is so other than us.

History and religion have conditioned us to view God as a demander, controller, ruthless, judgmental, black/white with no gray area, uncaring as to our circumstance and finally, downright mean at His core. Oh, and that personality is cloaked in a robe called love!

How bizarre that the former would be characterized by the latter. It is as if the statement, "Screw you because I love you" makes sense in this context. This kind of God would never be desired unless you were so scared of him you had a strategy to make friends with the playground bully in a quest for safety and protection.

But Isaiah seems to sense a different God than that. He seems to know, or perceive, the same God as Jesus portrayed, Paul promoted, John assured us of. Isaiah seems to know of a God that provides what we cannot procure, loves us when we are unlovable and promotes us when we should be ignored according to any merit system. And Isaiah seems to think that his partnership in the goals of God – justice for all – will inform people of the ways of God – righteousness.

Isaiah feels this to such a degree that he writes a verse to convey how "all in" he is – *"All night long, everything within me desires You."* When a new day dawns the core of who I am – my heart – will pursue you with desire.

Jeremiah seems to echo this idea of pursuing God being fulfilling when he writes in the voice of God, *"'you will call upon Me and go and pray to Me, and I will listen to you. And you will seek Me and find Me, when you search for Me with all your heart. I will be found by you', says the Lord."*

Have you ever, in your life, felt this way about God? That every time the sun comes up it is a new opportunity to pursue, seek, explore? In a reflection on this quest by Isaiah, Jesus comes along and says this, as if to underscore the necessity of desiring and pursuing God, *"All who keep asking will receive, all who keep seeking will find, and doors will open to those who keep knocking"* and *"Look, all of you are flawed in so many ways, yet in spite of all your faults, you know how to give good gifts to your children. How much more will your Father in heaven give the Holy Spirit to all who ask!"*

So, do you risk the opportunity for desiring God? Consider it.

27 *Make me hear of Your faithful love in the morning,*
for I trust in You.
Teach me how I should walk,
for I offer my soul up to You.
Psalm 142:8

Waking up to love. **What could be better?**

The original language used the term *'lovingkindness'* one of the world's most descriptive words of gentleness and care. The writer of this verse, David, was desperate and he knew the God he was talking to had kissed his days in the past. Now, he needed that God again.

David knew trouble and here it was again as many times before – facing a giant, a jealous King, a pregnant mistress, running from his son who was out to take his life and his throne – so he took to prayer. We do not want to delay prayer til panic, but we do want to analyze it so that we can see how to pray and how to manage our life when it's present!

The original language of this verse had David one step out of the grave in his own estimation. Hear his set up to his prayer…

I am begging, God.
Don't judge me or I'll be left short here.
I'm crushed by my enemy, living in the dark.
It's as if I am dead and gone, already, defeated.
I'm tired, weary and have nothing left.
My heart is depressingly empty.
But I remember the way it was.
You have done some big things
My hands are empty, so I am asking for your hands.
I am a desert in need of rain.

Now, THAT is pretty rough. Been there?

Then, three prayers in quick succession.

Hurry and answer me!
Rescue me from my enemies.
Bring me back to life.

When and how does David see the answer beginning to arrive to his soul?

In the morning.

New, fresh and hopeful opportunity must dawn in his life. And he makes a straightforward request – *"Make me hear of your faithful lovingkindness in the morning. Let's begin anew. Teach me how to walk with your direction. I'll follow you."*

David knows what you and I are now learning – for our lives to have life, we need the Father's opportunistic kiss in the morning and we need His guidance in the day.

Be honest with God about how you feel troubled and opportune your day with his lovingkindness.

A pure stream flows—never to be cut off— bringing joy to
the city where God makes His home,
the sacred site where the Most High chooses to live.
The True God never sleeps and always resides in
the city of joy; He makes it unstoppable, unshakable.
When it awakes at dawn,
the True God has already been at work.

The Sons of Korah, Psalm 46:4-5

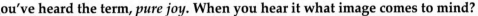

You've heard the term, *pure joy*. **When you hear it what image comes to mind?**

For me, it is the delight of a child that in a moment of abandoning everything else in the world, is in pure ecstasy; without any sense that there is any other thing happening than what is happening to them and bringing laughter, fulfillment, happiness and seclusion from everything but their present experience!

Now, how is that for a compound sentence!? Better, what would an opportunity like that mean to you?

This psalm of encouragement can recreate that feeling in an adult. It is an opportunity to trust God so deeply and closely that you live with him. I have learned so much of this kind of living from my mother: she has survived four fatal diseases, lived for decades after not being expected to live through the night, kept her address in God's City of Joy and will tell you all about how great and wonderful this City is, despite her seasons of suffering. When I was four, she survived *Guillain-Barré Syndrome*. When I was fifteen she was diagnosed with cancer. In my mid-thirties she visited my office to tell me she had been diagnosed with another aggressive cancer and would be having major surgery the next day. All three of these devastating diagnoses did not have a rescuable ending attached to them, yet she not only survived the diseases, but the horrible side-effects of the chemo and radiation therapies.

Finally, when I was 55, cancer came again, twice in five months. The second bout doubling the first in size and complexity. Doctors said that this form of cancer could not be stopped, only slowed. But, here we are six years later, and there is no sign or leftover luggage from that attack. All the while, she remained living at her same address – The City of Joy.

The verses that precede this invitation are all about the volume of fear that tries to drown out joy. The lyricist writes… *God is our shelter and our strength. When troubles seem near, God is nearer, and He's ready to help. So why run and hide?* No fear, no biting fingernails. When the earth spins out of control, we are sure and fearless. When the waters run wild, we are sure and fearless. In heavy winds, or as mountains shake, we are sure and fearless.

God loves us into joy if we relate, respond and retreat to Him. It's what inspired John, friend and Disciple of Jesus, to write – "*God is love. Anyone who lives faithfully in love also lives faithfully in God, and God lives in him… Love will never invoke fear. Perfect love expels fear, particularly the fear of punishment.*"

So, move on into the City of Joy: every dawn there is a fresh supply of opportunity.

29 *Get up early to sow your seed, and in the evening find worthwhile things to do, for you never know which will profit you—maybe this, maybe that, maybe both.*
Light is sweet; one glimpse of the sun delights the eyes.
Ecclesiastes 11:6-7

Opportunities.

Sometimes they pan out, and sometimes they do not. But every day they are there.

What is the greatest opportunity you have ever had that you missed and wished you had it back? Or, what is the greatest opportunity seized?

The opportunities I have had and taken define me, create my story, color my life – no matter if they were successful or not. The ones I haven't taken, who knows? Of the ones I have taken I have traveled to four continents, met thousands of people, spoken on platforms I'd never known about, had totally impactful encounters and experienced moments that are indelibly written on my heart.

I do not wonder much about the ones I passed on, but that doesn't mean I haven't wondered. At those times, I compare and ask, "Would I trade what I know for what I do not know?" And the answer every time is "*No!*"

I have heard of bad opportunities. I remember a friend of mine invited me to his home to see his latest, greatest opportunity. When I arrived we went down to his basement where he had plant lights installed and a lot of small aquarium type glass cubes with 4"-6" green shoots abounding. Then he told me about how that he would expand from here and how many billions of dollars were spent on high-end perfumes each year and how he'd be a major supplier of this particular plant necessary in the production of alluring fragrances.

I know exactly what you are thinking, and you are correct… no way. Within a few months, when those huge multi-national corporations that produce those fragrant scents that grace the wrists and necks of alluring women the world over did not come calling, the basement was cleared out.

But the promise remains, and this is where I almost get giddy sometimes: "*Light is sweet. A glimpse of the sun delights the eyes.*" That is the treasure of opportunity. Today you have one, maybe more than one, and you have a chance to "*Sow your seed, because you never know…*"

Can you imagine what your opportunity might be today? What you will sow into it? How you will be ready to recognize it when the door opens?

Every opportunity may not be in business. What if you have an opportunity to sow goodness into a person you love and care for? What might be the return on investment? What if you see an opportunity for goodness that has been created because of a circumstance of difficulty for someone you meet, or already know? What light of change will you be to their life today? What organization that is working diligently to make a difference will you invest in today knowing that your investment's payoff will be for someone down the line because you paid it forward?

Get a glimpse of your sunlight today… and meet it with delight.

30

*At first the earth lacked shape and was totally empty,
and a dark fog draped over the deep while God's spirit-
wind hovered over the surface of the empty waters.
Then there was the voice of God. "Let there be light."
And light flashed into being. God saw that the light was
beautiful and good, and He separated the light from the
darkness. God named the light "day" and the darkness
"night." Evening gave way to morning. That was day one.*
Genesis 1:1

The first day.

We have a lot of first days in our life. The first day of existence. The first day of school. The first day of parenthood. The first day of marriage. The first day after a tragedy has changed the context of our life. The first day of faith. The first day of doubt. I totally grasp the meaning of *a first day*.

Have you ever noticed the choice of words the author of this Creation account utilized about the first day? Look at it with me…"*Evening gave way to morning. That was day one.*"

All of us have dark times, night seasons of our experience of life, but the message to our souls about God speaking creatively over us is this – evening gave way to morning. That is the language of opportunity.

In another morning contemplation we saw the message of the Psalmist that "*The deepest pains may linger through the night, but joy greets the soul with the smile of morning.*"

As I write this, I am waiting for a new day to come. I am waiting for a new manifestation of life, provision and abundance. The scope and nature of this new thing is beyond my ability to produce on my own, so I am summoning joy to lift my thinking beyond my predicament.

Joy is a fruit, a product, of the recreated human spirit alive in relationship to its Creator. Joy is an upload from our spirit, deep within the abode of God, Holy Spirit, to our soul – our mind, will and emotional being. Joy is strength when it comes from the gift of God's presence in us. That is why the ancient texts, written by people aware and in touch with the Divine, encourage us to re-visit, re-new, re-fill with joy… "*Most of all, friends, always rejoice in the Lord! I never tire of saying it: Rejoice!*"

Jesus, in the most difficult of his days on Earth, was sentenced to death, yet He did not lose His focus on Joy. We are pointed to look at, consider His way, he "*endured the cross and ignored the shame of that death because He focused on the joy that was set before Him; and now He is seated beside God.*" It was a once-in-a-lifetime opportunity that Jesus did not pass up. His acceptance of the opportunity gives us new opportunities. It really is *new every morning*.

This book is meant to be read again and again, as needed or wanted, on the mornings your soul is waking and seeking the opportunity of new hope, new vision, new thought and new design for life. Always remember – "*Evening gave way to morning. That was day one.*"

Go have your new Day One.

NOTES

....

....

....

....

....

....

....

....

....

....

....

....

....

....

....

....

New Every Morning
An Experience in Opportunity

I want to be your partner in this reflection on the opportunities God affords humanity every day. There are three specific ways for your and I to journey forward together.

1. Download your personal companion guide at philunderwood.com to further seed your thoughts, prayer and actions to seize what is before you, for your good. This daily response guide to the reflection will help you optimize your experience.
2. Join Phil's personal online community at facebook.com/epicfaithonline for a continuous offering of inspiration and engagement in spiritual focus and life design.
3. Share this book on your social media, give as gifts to people you want to encourage and please post a review at Amazon.com - https://bit.ly/UnderwoodReview

Phil Underwood
phil@philunderwood.com

About the Author

Phil Underwood is a son of the south. Raised in Atlanta, Georgia in the midst of racial integration, cultural shift and gender awareness, he is an eclectic pot of old and new, worse and better, godly and worldly, weird and accepted.

Phil is the father of three amazingly gifted daughters, Andrea, Alexis and Amanda, extra dad to Andy and Wihan, Darren and Candace & Drew, Opa to Gemma, Levi and Phoebe, G to Elliott and Emory. But, we are sure there are more to come for this roster.

Committed to a non-religious relationship with Jesus Christ, Phil lives to share, model and invite others into this divine pathway – humanity's original purpose – reigning in life by grace and redeeming love.

Phil would love to hear from you and invites you to get in touch anytime – **phil@philunderwood.com.**

I want to invite you to my place in paradise, The Florida Keys.

The Keys are an archipelago of coral isles off the southern coast of Florida, beginning near Miami and reaching over 125 miles in a southwestern swag direction ending in the world famous Key West, home to such luminaries as Ernest Hemingway, Shel Silverstein, Tennessee Williams, Judy Blum and Jimmy Buffett. It was also the retreat for U.S. President Harry Truman and others.

Stretching from the northernmost populace of Key Largo, through Islamorada, Marathon, Big Pine Key and then to Key West, The Keys boast the only living coral reef in the United States, one of the world's most popular underwater diving spots. Islamorada is known as The Sport Fishing Capital of the World. Marathon is home to the Seven Mile Bridge built to host the first railroad, and land based transportation through The Keys, The Flagler Railroad. From there, find the diminutive and rare Key Deer on Big Pine, the sleepy and quiet Saddle Bunch Keys and then Key West.

So diverse from region to region – upper, middle and lower Keys – everyone can find a place to commune with nature and enjoy the relaxation available in my part of the world. I even have a guest house I provide for individuals and couples wanting 3-5 day spiritual and reflective retreats that include visiting The Reef, great food, and easy-going kayaking, paddle boarding and fishing.

Visit our paradise & enjoy life… *New Every Morning!*

Phil Underwood

Explore Our Keys Paradise…

https://fla-keys.com
https://islamoradachamber.com
https://www.keylargochamber.org
https://marathonflorida.com
https://www.lowerkeyschamber.com
https://keywest.com